FENCES

THE DREAMSEEKER
POETRY SERIES

Books in the DreamSeeker Poetry Series, intended to make available fine writing by Anabaptist-related poets, are published by Cascadia Publishing House under the DreamSeeker Books imprint and sometimes have been copublished with Herald Press. Cascadia oversees content of these poetry collections in collaboration with DreamSeeker Poetry Series Editor Jeff Gundy (Jean Janzen volumes 1-4) as well as when called for in consultation with its Editorial Council and the authors themselves.

Also worth noting are two poetry collections that would likely have been included in the series had it been in existence then:

1 Empty Room with Light
   By Ann Hostetler, 2002

2 A Liturgy for Stones
   By David Wright, 2003

DreamSeeker Books also continues to release an occasional high-caliber collection of poems outside of the DreamSeeker Poetry Series:

1 The Mill Grinds Fine: Collected Poems
   By Helen Wade Alderfer, 2009

2 How Trees Must Feel
   By Chris Longenecker, 2011

FENCES

Poems by
Cheryl Denise

DreamSeeker Poetry Series, Volume 20

DreamSeeker Books
TELFORD, PENNSYLVANIA

an imprint of
Cascadia Publishing House LLC

Cascadia Publishing House orders, information, reprint permissions:
contact@CascadiaPublishingHouse.com
1-215-723-9125
126 Klingerman Road, Telford PA 18969
https://www.CascadiaPublishingHouse.com

Library of Congress Cataloging-in-Publication Data

Names: Denise, Cheryl, 1965- author.
Title: Fences / poems by Cheryl Denise.
Description: Telford, Pennsylvania : DreamSeeker Books, 2022. | Series: The
    Dreamseeker poetry series ; volume 20 | Summary: "This collection offers
    poems about fences and boundaries and borders--whether keeping the
sheep
    in or maintaining or breaking the fences the author puts up around self,
    marriage, friendships, the greater world"-- Provided by publisher.
Identifiers: LCCN 2022037408 | ISBN 9781680270235 (trade paperback)
Subjects: LCGFT: Poetry.
Classification: LCC PS3604.E585 F46 2022 | DDC 811/.6--
dc23/eng/20220808
LC record available at https://lccn.loc.gov/2022037408

27 26 25 24 23 22   10 9 8 7 6 5 4 3 2 1

With thanks to good friends and fellow writers:
Carol Del Col, Barbara Smith and Sandy Vrana,
who have enriched my poetry and my life.

For the people I come from:
my grandparents,
Gladys and Norman B. Martin
Lydia Ann and Howard S. Bauman

my mom and dad,
Isabel and Jim Bauman

and for Mike, whom I would marry again

CONTENTS

FENCES II

FENCES III

WHERE I'M FROM

WHERE I'M FROM

I'm from clotheslines off back porches,
from pickle brine and cook cheese
from a mother who made us kids sniff horseradish
at the first sign of a cold.

I'm from shape notes, knitting needles
and pickling corn,
ink stains and silver typeset,
Dad's Heidelberg press forever snorting
like a stallion in the old chicken coop.

From neighbor kids flooding the backyard for hockey
imagining ourselves as Wayne Gretzky and Bobby Orr.

From a giant white Bible on a coffee table
with a picture of Solomon about to split a baby in two.

I'm from home-sewn bathing suits, accordion lessons,
breaking curfew and smoking Players,
Gloria Vanderbilt jeans and Farrah Fawcett hair.

From a mother who had two dates in one night,
a father who snuck out of the parsonage
to see *South Pacific* at that verboten
movie house.

From a grandfather who refused to go to war,
sent west to fight forest fires instead
while his wife gave birth on a poultry farm.

I'm from recycled ancestors—
the ones I can't name
and don't understand, but who somehow
survive in my bones, grounding me here,
to this place where I'm from.

THE GIRL INSIDE THE WOMAN

I live in a tall house,
on Church Street, in Elmira, in Canada.
Our flag is hard to draw.
Fifteen wooden steps
creak to our part of the house.
I don't know my right from my left
and when I grow up
I want to be a cowgirl.
The old man who lives below
rakes his thin hair up
and rolls it like hay.
He lets me talk to his goldfish.

Mom reads Rapunzel
and makes cream peas and scalloped potatoes.
I have a new sister; she smells like milk
and doesn't do much. Soon
we will get an even smaller baby and need a bigger
house. But first Mom will get sick and Dad scared
and I will spend my days in Beatrice's basement.
She has an Easy-Bake Oven and a teenage boy
I will fall in love with and never talk to.

In the dark part of our house
a freezer whines and a baby buggy
sits in the corner like a bad girl. The walls
hover cool and gray; no one stays in here long except
the cat and me.

Every morning Dad bikes uphill to work.
I push the cat in the black buggy but never
reach his shop. I am not supposed to go
that far.

The cat is the same color as the sun
rolled in dirt.
She is thin as a sunflower stalk and almost as long.
She scratches me, wrist to shoulder,
when I dress her in doll clothes.
I am not allowed to dress up my sister.

People tell me how beautiful my baby is,
wrapped in a soft blanket.
We all know she is a cat, but no one says so.
Then one day she leaps from the buggy
and heads to the woods, never to come back.

Decades later
I'm still that girl,
climbing hills part way only,
pretending.

RECURRING DREAM

A thousand grey grasshoppers
carpet my front lawn.
I'm seven once more

alone by the evergreen
on the far edge of the grass
and no way to reach the front door.

A wet green stench rolls towards me,
robotic hind legs click against leathery wings.
Every blade a launching pad, a tiny trampoline.

Fabre's Book of Insects says
The White-faced Decticus
is fond of biting.

Like my ballet teacher
silver hair pulled tight as commandments
demanding perfect pirouettes.

Like Carl in the playground,
too old for grade school,
guarding the monkey bars.

If that grasshopper
gets hold of your finger
he can make the blood come.

Broad-faced and dull of intellect,
they cut the nerves so their prey can't move—
and they won't let me go home.

RUNNING GIRL

Grade six at my new school,
I join the cross-country team.
We run the first half hour of lunch
then get the *whole* cafeteria to ourselves.
David, the boy who will ask me to be his partner
for square dancing in gym, plays "The Bumble Boogie,"
faster and faster, his fingers racing the piano
as we hustle trades from our Peanuts,
Barbie and Incredible Hulk lunch boxes.

Soon I will break a record for the girls,
the most kilometers run in the school year.
It shouldn't count. I hate the cafeteria at noon,
the soggy spitballs, the boys who talk engines,
wrestling, cutting class,
the redhead siren with her streak of grey.

I jog to be alone and
to make the boy who will run the most kilometers
want me as his girlfriend. He won't.

Soon Terry Fox with one real leg and one fake
will dip his wooden foot in the Atlantic
at St. John's Newfoundland and begin
his cross-Canada run for cancer,
his awkward double-step and hop.
My family will huddle in the rain in Sudbury cheering
     before he stops in Thunder Bay
               and the whole country grieves.

In high school, I will never win a race
and the record-breaking boy will not notice me
but I'll still run my legs long and lean,
mind wandering free.
I'll run to get out of class early on Fridays,
to ride the bus to some rival school,
to belong to a team of friends who like me fast or slow.

And I still run, decades later,
for that last kilometer, for the journey home,
believing again what we knew those nights
stomping and clapping, singing "We Are the Champions,"
loud as the bus driver would bear.

INHERITANCE

After Uncle Ken shot himself
Mom bought us an organ with the money he left.
She heard laughter in the blue cha cha
and red rumba buttons.
I heard old folks moaning
hymns in front pews.
    Surely Ken never meant to punish us.
He wore bell-bottoms and looked like disco,
read us the comics,
gave us an orange stuffed hippo covered with daisies.

Before the organ, the accordion
because lessons were offered just across the street
at the Canadian Legion.
    As if middle-school wasn't hard enough.
Not getting a part in *Chicken Little*,
breaking the bandsaw in shop,
and evenings playing hide-and-seek.
Mom calling from the porch,
Time for your accordion lesson!

Then I heard the magnificent
Jimmy Holmstrom playing the organ
for the Toronto Maple Leafs, perched
above the rink like a god
orchestrating the fans, ordering us
to yell *Charge.*

And years later in New Orleans on Bourbon
Street, my hips discovered zydeco,
its old-world accordion stretching
and folding the night.

But I quit both the organ and the accordion
unable to imagine they could bring me happiness
like so many other things I inherited
    and let go.

IGNITION

The first time he came to my house
I was downstairs applying a second coat
of Maybelline's Great Lash,
the kind Christie Brinkley wore.
When I emerged he was lounging at the table
with a slice of grape pie on a Corelle plate,
my mother rambling about the Sugar Kings' game.

The first time I went to his place he tried to warn me
but I didn't hear until the house sighed and slanted
sparse as a drawing from a Grimm fairytale.
The floor uneven and crumbling, the smell of wet dog.
No welcome from his mother; I was nothing to her.
On a couch lumpy as a feed sack, we ate Jiffy pop
and watched *Fantasy Island*.

I thought poverty was another country.
After that we were always at my place
or the Chinese restaurant or Morty's Pub.

In the green and black velvet hallway
of my parents' home, he murmured,
Everything a man could want,
as if he'd forgotten me, his eyes wandering
the fake gold framed mirror and candle sconces,
the living room's plush carpet, the organ,
the bowls of hard candy and mixed nuts.

I miss him, his red hair, his dreams of leaving,
becoming a bartender or anything
his mom disapproved of.
I miss his orange Pinto,
the way he grinned when I cried *Mercy*
in that death trap, the gas tank in back,
everything dangerous and ready to explode.

BORDERS

At the border between past and future
no caution signs advise slippery roads ahead,
slow down, make a U-turn when safe.
No rheumy-eyed cop waits at Wagner's Corner
cocks his head through the window and warns:
>   *You know when you come back*
>   *everything's going to be the same*
>   *but you'll feel like a traitor.*

But already you've gassed it down the QEW
along with all the other jalopies, hotrods & minivans—
three lanes of traffic, horns, exhaust fumes.
Tractor trailers block signs for off ramps:
you couldn't change course if you tried.

You crest the Sky Bridge,
a new horizon beckons
like a lost friend you never had
and you think, surely, she will help you find yourself.

So you ignore the final duty-free shop
stuffed with maple leaf souvenirs you'll want later.
And now you wait in line
while that German Shepherd that lunged at you as a kid
circles your rusty Toyota.

Then suddenly Carl, the bully from grade two
bounds out of a booth: *Anything to declare?*
You want to say your freedom, a sovereign mind;
but a joke could send you back
to your childhood.

And now you're winding up a gravel road
living on a community farm,
chasing sheep, raising chicks,
fixing poetry in the college basement
with an English prof, a cross-dresser,
and a preacher who writes science fiction.

It bothers you that people here
leave their shoes on in the house,
admit they're hungry when asked only once,
that no one makes butter tarts
or goes curling Friday nights.

Years pass: still some days you ache
for walks that lead to your sister's flowerbeds.

When you hear plans for the new arena
you dream of an invitation to come home,
read your hockey poem.
Your old schoolmates will stomp and howl.

You imagine all they remember
is the girl who failed grade two,
who later rinsed diapers in the hopper
at the nursing home when it seemed
everyone else was a rising Malcolm Gladwell.

But even though you unfurled and became bold,
reading poems on the radio,
still some days, roaming these hills,
you wish for a family crisis,
an unexpected surgery,

anything to pull you north for a month,
    maybe two,
pretending you could stay.

FENCES

FENCES

In spring I dream of woven wire gleaming
with sunlight and promises kept,
fresh silver pulled taut against long lines
of locust posts erect as soldiers
alert and ready.

But my fence is a reunion of droopy old men
barely able to hang on to their tangle of rusty wires.

This morning five lambs hopped over
the sagging strands, dashed up the gravel road.
7:20 a.m. and me dressed for the office
and the neighbor in work boots
calling from his porch,
Cheryl, you need help?
I always need help.

Two farms over, Freddie's fence is worse,
cows loose every few weeks, grazing
our front field. His cell phone never works
so I have to call his mother.
     It takes a few days
before his rusty Chevy careens up the drive,
Freddie's head out the window, hand on the horn
herding his thin Jerseys back to their steep
grassless pasture.

Sometimes when my fence is working
I sit inside it as if part of the flock.
Wool-clouds drift by on pipe-cleaner legs.
A ewe sniffs my boots,
stares into my eyes, the rectangle bars of her pupils
supposing me something exotic.
As if on a dare two lambs climb my coveralls
nibble the shiny buttons, then race off
to play tag with the rest
sprinting from one sturdy
fence line to the other.

As if hearing some wild good news
silver-wooled Edna surveys the sky
leaps sideways three times kicking her heels.
Then stops
        looks left,
                checks right,
hoping her companions didn't see.

She scurries to join them,
content to munch the grass of this field.

WAKING TO SPRING

I've been collecting words for years
for this exact day—
the sun spread thick over the land
thick as Dad butters his toast
as if butter is better than bread, than earth.

The pond quiet as an unopened story
since the red-haired boy shot wide
to shoo two beavers.

See the quaking maple leaves,
branches bobbing, *Yes, Yes, Yes.*
And the buttercups in the tall grass telling me
Be beautiful.

My golden retriever with grey-rimmed eyes—
yesterday we sheared him with the sheep.
Feel he is softer now, younger.
And I still have a little childhood inside.
Red Rover, Red Rover, let Cheryl come over.

In the field with the fence yet unbroken
the spotted Jacob sheep walk single file
on spindly stalks, down to the spring-fed trough.

See the newest lamb
hopping straight up,
left   and   right,
as if the ground is full of coiled springs—
look, her umbilical cord
        still dangling.

CALLING IN SICK

We get no mental health days
and since Zoloft is a lie
I'm telling my boss I've a headache.

I can't take another day without poetry

and I need to call my sister in Ontario
    talk long
    find out how she really is.

I yearn to hike in the woods
listen to what the trees say
watch a family of turkeys
then describe them to my 105-year-old Grandma.

But first I must retrieve my notebook
and my fast pen.
A poem clamors to be written.
I can hear the metaphors
knocking at the door.

Self-Appraisal

When I slip it on my finger a second time
I decide I'll buy it,
even though I want the more expensive opal.

I choose the moment to show my husband.
He says it looks like an eyeball
with a loose lower lid
— and it does.
He asks how much
and the lie slides out fast,
easy. The turquoise stone pretty
even if fake like those baubles in middle school,
the cool girls dangled from their necks on silver chains
while skipping double-dutch
Ladybug, ladybug, turn around
Ladybug, ladybug, touch the ground.

For two weeks I pack my lunch
count how much I saved
by not eating at Subway. When I tell my husband
it's paid for, he says I shouldn't beat myself up.
But in the first years of marriage,
when money was tight, and pizza a luxury,
we would have asked,
Is the ring worth four pizzas?

In high school I saved
most of my clothing allowance,
afraid of adulthood,
of budgets and bills.
Eventually Mom bought me Gloria Vanderbilt
jeans and a red knit dress with shoulder pads.
Even in my thirties she gave me an L.L. Bean coat
so I wouldn't wear my barn jacket to church.

I think of Grandma eating the cheapest
thing on the menu while Grandpa orders steak.
She never wears jewelry
I can't imagine her wanting beauty for herself.
My husband replaces his cross-country skis
but I'm sure I can get another season out of mine.
The following winter he so easily glides past me
through the pines.

Money is the root of all evil
I say, but my sister corrects me,
It's the love of money.
But it's hard to have money you don't love.

I slip the ring on awkward and heavy
finger the silver feathers that cradle
the stone, not precious, not quite beautiful
wishing I bought that opal instead,
imagining it on the fingers of the now grown women
from recess, strutting down Main Street
humming to themselves.

EARLY MORNING IN THE BARN

Newborn lamb
face swathed in mucus,
chest flat and still, legs splayed,
mother uselessly licking her side.

I grasp her hind legs
    swing her in an arc
again and again as if on a ride at the fair
and just like that kid that let go
a stomach of cotton
candy and corn dogs
she spews the white phlegm
    gasps
and I give her back to her mother.

It worked
just as it said it would in
Raising Sheep the Modern Way,
written in 1976,
a gift from Dennis who said,
Read this, we'll raise sheep,
start a community, what can go wrong?

But so much did. Wells went dry,
the driveway washed out, lightning struck
the tractor shed, the sheep escaped
to wander with the neighbor's Holsteins
a whole summer.

At our meeting every fall
Dennis suggests we keep raising sheep
or each just flush $200 down the toilet.
It saves on property taxes, I offer.
I can't explain
how those noisy wool bodies soften me,
like a margarita after work.

That lamb went to market
or escaped in the woods
was eaten by coyotes or dogs
or maybe made it to motherhood
and is chewing her cud in the barn.

I never learned her markings,
never named her,
the only thing I ever saved.

Coming Home from Jail

Thanks for the ride,
after I sell my truck I'll pay the back rent,
I'll be gone by the end of the month.

Four months later, no rent,
truck not sold, not running.
I help him load boxes,
move four truckloads of furniture.
Next day his mother comes by, cleans the windows.

Before Him

My daughter forgot about the hillside
and smashed into the porch with my car.
It's not that bad really.

I'll pay you the last month's rent
after I start my new job in Florida.

While Advertising

I'm calling about your place on Maple.
My house burned down,
my fiancé lit a candle in the bedroom,
he blew it out
but the fire marshal isn't convinced.
He's a heart transplant and forgetful

I'm worried he'll leave the stove on.
I'm trying to get on at Sheetz.
I've got good references.

THE PASTOR WHO PLAYS THE HARP

asks if we'd rent our place to a family
who desperately needs a home.
She'll vouch for them
and the church can help, some.

A year later the father tries transitioning
to a woman, red nail polish,
longish hair, the ends dyed pink,
a sequined T-shirt riding above
a mountainous white belly.

While fixing the water heater
my husband listens,
tries to be understanding
as the dad talks of miracles,
how he's developing breasts
without hormones or treatment.

Eventually his wife kicks him out
and there he is muttering to himself
on the bench outside the IGA,
the police talking him down.
Ends up in the mental ward.
His wife and kids take off without notice,
without the last two months' rent
and no forwarding address.
Leaving behind two truckloads
of mismatched shoes, frayed sweatshirts
and a Boy Scout compass.

Chicken fat on the living room walls,
sparkled lip gloss smeared in the carpet,
a twenty-five-pound oxygen tank,
melted popsicles stuck behind the fridge
and in bedroom closets.

The pastor knows another family.

The Boy from Down the Hill

Age 6 races up the snowy woods,
jacket unzipped, boots untied,
yelling *Cheryl, Cheryl, I got you a Christmas card,*
      waving it high as he can,
after I baked his family whoopie pies for the holidays.

Age 7 telling stories at the bonfire
until my ninety-pound mutt steals his sausage.
Should I put the dog in the house, I ask, *sorry he's a bully.*
No, I gave him my sandwich, I'm not hungry,
he insists while petting the dog,
standing as far from him as possible.
I roast two more, he eats both while I hold the thief.

Age 9 learns to smoke behind a round hay bale
with his older brother, before running across the field
hollering, *We gotta tell 'em!*
Bucket after bucket of water,
we load the pick-up, the burnt smell rising.
Takes three days for that bale to smolder to nothing.

Age 13 carves R.S. ♥ M.C.
in the bark of my husband's tree stand.

Age 14 grinning, wears his football uniform
home from school,
walks a mile from the bus stop to his shot-up trailer,
bounds up the steps, knocking over the driveshaft
that props up the porch roof.

Age 15 jimmies the lock on Earl's back door,
steals a TV, a jar of loose change.
Earl asks him to pay it off in yard work, feeds him lunch.
No police, no reports.

Age 16 roughs up an elderly man over some weed.
His mom says she didn't raise him like that.
Three months in a tough love camp.

Age 17 Mom in jail.
A HAZMAT team in the yard.
A dismantled meth lab.

Age 18 pictured on the front page
of the Barbour Democrat,
blank stare, shaggy hair,
in the regional jail for cooking meth.

Age 19 hit with a crowbar by his older brother.
I hear this on the scanner at the beauty shop.

Age 20 shows me pictures of his two kids on his cell phone,
they live with their mothers. And he still lives with his,
in the trailer, no heat, no electricity,
black garbage bags over the roof.

Age 22 Sheriff staked out by my hay barn
in the early dark, then running, yelling—
but two nights later I hear that generator again.

<u>Age 24</u> I pick him up hitchhiking,
ripped jeans, beer-breathed,
his face a plowed field, dirt and stone,
but I see that six-year-old,
his full name scrawled across the manger.

PROPHETS

In 1853 Jonas Stutzman builds a giant chair for Jesus
to set up office in Holmes County, Ohio.
When Jesus does not come,
Jonas renounces earthly time and
throws his grandfather clock in the pigsty.

Since he is harmless and without disciples
the Old Orders keep him in church, an errant child.
They help construct new stalls for his sows.
He wears nothing but white, hat to shoes,
ready to greet Christ when the trumpet sounds.
At his funeral, the Old Orders
respect his fear of wheels and
carry his casket three miles to the church.

In 2018 my cousin Tom climbs Eagle's Peak
to witness the second coming, waiting for Christ
to appoint him the highest honor of Heaven.
When Jesus does not show,
Tom renounces earthly wealth and
becomes homeless.

We Mennonites try to help him
but our worldly therapists and hospitals are useless.
He gives freely to beggars, claims cancer of the soul.
At his memorial we do not speak of his visions.

The Old Orders kept Jonas alive for eighteen years.
We could not keep Tom for one,

shunning the fearsome faith, the unending farm work
that might have kept Tom with us,
as he was in the beginning
and should have been forevermore,
a bit crazy, sure, but hilarious,
handing out Mardi Gras beads and cowboy hats,
celebrating the birth of another day.

CHOSEN BY LOT

for my grandfather

Sunday morning March 25th, 1945
a red brick Mennonite Church
the foyer hosting a long line of black boots
    dripping.
Above in the jaundiced sanctuary
    a wooden cross
and sunlight slanting in narrow windows
women and children on the left   men on the right
    almost every pew brimming
the faint smell of Holsteins and hogs,
the anticipation thick as locust honey.

A month earlier the bishop had knocked,
told Howard the congregation picked him and one other,
would he be willing to cast his name?

Now the bishop beckons the two men forward
before a table set with three Bibles
(three in case God deems neither man fit for the call)
only one hides a slip of paper
a blank white rectangle
with the power to invoke a preacher from a man.

Eight years in, the congregation buys a parsonage,
moves Howard off the farm and into town
where there's room for only a small garden, a relief
from the huge field, the insistent work.
Howard reads scripture on the banks of the Grand,

hears God as a river
    rushing, smoothing,
    washing away the old.

Pacing sermons loud and sturdy
he plows the fields of his congregation
shovels the soil of redemption and feeds his flock.

The rewards are heavenly but the pay paltry.
He has six children and a wife
so he builds a chicken coop,
buys a small printer for his sons' bedroom
where market flyers and hockey tickets churn.

Now his earthly body rests behind the church,
a maple planted in his honor grows by the river,
and the chicken coop, turned into Bauman Printing,
stables a snorting, heaving Heidelberg press.
His flock, now scattered, wonders
if they found their callings
    —their slips of paper
slid between God's words.

Trust and Obey
Grandma sings in the front row,
ninety-seven, straight backed,
soprano belief rising like incense from her narrow
sanctuary, right hand resting on Grandpa's wooden cane.
But I hear those doubts she wrote in her journals
whispering from that shoebox
she said we could open and read,
—doubts which she always turned, rushing explanations
        landing on sturdy scriptures,

for there's no other way
to live with a preacher
who lost two mothers
the first catching fire at the cook stove
apron ablaze, running, rolling, rolling in the yard
and the second a hired housekeeper
walking out when he was twelve,
no explanation, the kitchen empty
when he came home from school.
It's all she can do

to be happy in Jesus
when her son, Ken, asked why she had so many kids;
when they lived five weeks in a basement
and she cooked on a hot plate.
When Ken took his life at twenty.
Nothing

but to trust and obey
in those absurdly thin pages
even when Grandpa faltered,
when his hair turned orange
one Saturday at the barber shop back in 1962,
when hair dye was as confounding as Leviticus,
who that Sunday preached without the lights on
afterwards vanished through the side door
quick as a miracle,
leaving Grandma to shake hands, to make excuses,
to comfort him when she got home.
And when Grandpa had his breakdown she still trusted
even when he ordered her to hush six children,
to forever have supper ready five o'clock sharp.

When we walk with the Lord
do we have to pretend everything will turn to glory
in the end? Does Grandma believe
because we, her family, need her to?
Does she remember those journals and is she waiting
to be asked, wanting to speak plainly,
trusting our love to hold
knowing there's another way?

A SCRIPT OF SEVEN DAYS

Listen, women
when contempt changed the god story,
a garden grew, a rib was pulled.
Greed and discontentment slid
a snake in the grass, hung
an apple crisp and low
    delicious
            thought Eve
hungry after pruning paradise all day.
When the snake spoke
she thought it was the one from Canaan
who gave wisdom to the goddess,
so Eve listened, plucked and bit
and women all around the globe
swallowed
    the sweet juice
            men named the sin.

Before the god of Moses
a whirling goddess rocked a cradled valley
where we planted and gathered beside the men.
Everyone sated.
In summer we strolled naked
and glorious while irises bloomed.
The snake, *life of earth*,
shed papery scrolls and roamed free.
Each morning the sun opened
the hills, and we woke
fearless, under a blue sky
with no god to blame us
for bringing evil to the world.

NOT A BEDTIME STORY

that one where God orders Abraham
to slay his son Isaac

and without argument
Abraham saddles up his donkey

and Isaac, giddy with excitement,
talks nonstop, happy to be chosen
to trek up the mountain with his father.

Not until preparing for worship
does Isaac think to ask where the lamb is.

Did some verses go missing?
Next thing you read, Abraham is tying
his son on the altar, raising the knife.

Perhaps he hesitates,
just long enough for God to glance into
the twenty-first century where
a devout Christian mother shudders in disgust.

So God decides to cut his losses,
squares his shoulders, straightens his beard,
and summons an angel to yell, "Stop."

Who can blame Isaac for his future blunders,
risking his wife's virtue for his safety,
giving his eldest boy a blessing of violence and drought,
like Abraham, botching up his son's psyche.
  Like God.

WHEN YOU WENT AWAY

the earth darkened,
people looked at their feet,
started home.

Some say you spent three days
in the belly of the earth
with the old archangel.

Before this you raised Lazarus,
after four days.
You cannot be four days in a tomb just sleeping
unlike the little girl *dead*
for an hour or so.

God left you,
left all of us, the jeering mocking crowd,
with global warming and suicide bombers.

In Jesus Christ Superstar they end with the crucifixion,
no disco dancing garden scene for Sunday morning
just a tired Friday night bus heading back to before.

Last Easter I asked
my girlfriend, and she said she has to believe
in resurrection, she's a gardener.

Now it's happening again.
The tiny birdhouse I built fills
with five big bluebirds,

and there by the cut stone chimney
      circles of daffodils trumpet through the snow,
while above, my neighbor,
nineteen and needing a new kidney
      crests the hill on his four-wheeler
persistent as the sun.

THE FIRST GAY WEDDING IN THE GODSHALL FAMILY

The Save the Date card's edged with gold glitter
that doesn't rub off,
doesn't stick to your fingers,
or scatter across the table and floor.
I never knew they could make it so practical,
so jubilant, Jason and Rocco in blue winter coats,
a kiss on the cheek.

Sally, Jason's Mom, wants to pay for our hotel,
maybe because we don't believe the Bible condemns
homosexuality, maybe because we live simply
and so she thinks we're poor.
Either way we're happy to go, but nervous,
we don't own nice clothes.
Chandeliers, fine china and small talk scare us.

Black Tie Optional.
We're Mennonite,
the quiet in the land,
not long ago we thought buttons too worldly.

In the 1960's Great Grandma supported divorcees
becoming church members,
but later wondered if that opened the door too wide.
But she loved Jason enough to question
her understanding of scripture.

I think the apostle Paul was gay and frustrated.
My father-in-law disagrees.

Still he will come, grateful for the invitation,
as we all are, knowing Jesus wants everyone
to come to the banquet
     even if you just bought a cow
     or have fields and commitments
or belong to a church without
a rainbow-colored dove on the door.

When Jason was five my husband taught him
how to use the word *ominous.*
When he was nine, he played whiffle ball with me
my first time at Men-o-lan meeting the Godshall clan.
When he was a teenager, he sang
in Christopher Dock's touring choir.
On the blurred cover of the CD you can pick him out
by his red hair.
Mike swears he can hear Jason's voice cradling the rest.

We met Rocco once at a family picnic.
He came late, left early, whisking Jason away
to a Katy Perry concert.
Maybe we scared him.

Nine months to go and already I'm worried
about my husband's shoes.
I haven't even replaced my good bra
that the washing machine ruined last month.
What will I do with my Olive Oyl figure?
I can't borrow a dress from any of my friends
none of them are tall, flat-chested,
straight hipped with big feet.

My husband asks Carla at the thrift store
to watch the donations. She power-smiles,
assures him she'll make him look dapper
like Matthew McConaughey in those Lexus commercials.

Black Tie Optional.
My husband Googles it.
It gets scarier.
His long grey beard implies
free thinking, non-conformity.
I refused a white wedding,
knit him a sweater.
Our invitation said dress casual
square dancing and table games after the ceremony.

There'll be a real dance at this wedding
not the kind you have in a barn.
Dancing used to be verboten for Mennonites
and still is in some circles.
That's why I love it
and Mike dreads it.
No one taught us how to feel music in our hips.
Growing up church elders liked our bodies straight
as plowed fields, perfect rows of corn and wheat,
the boys in a separate plot from the girls.

Sally, reassuring as cake,
says there won't be any fashion police,
nor dance judges.
But it's more than that.
We came from immigrants, from farms.

We worshiped in caves, were burned at the stake,
left Germany and Switzerland
fled in trains, on boats.
They called us milksops
and now it's okay to dress like orchids?
This after Great Great Grammy near the end
in the hospital
said she didn't cut her hair for pride.
But even she wore a lavish hat and stylish dress
in her youth.

In the 18th century we fled to America
to avoid persecution,
but time has passed and maybe now it's okay
to pursue a little happiness, a little success,
celebrate Jason and Rocco.

So we'll laugh at our awkwardness,
use the wrong spoon, dance as if we look good.

Jason and Rocco welcome us all
to indulge in the extravagance, the harvest
we forgot was for everyone
        even us.

BORDER CROSSING

It was supposed to be intoxicating
and romantic—
from the beaded engagement ring
to the square dance after the ceremony
to our 50th anniversary.

But before the wedding Mom spent six weeks
on hold, long distance with the American Consulate.

I think the US government scouts for future officers
early at elementary school playgrounds,
finds the bullies studying the fine art of bloody noses.

I had to get a police record
saying I have no police record.

My future in-laws sent tax returns,
signed forms saying they'd support me
if their son couldn't.

We honeymooned in Toronto
spent each morning in line outside
that miserable grey bricked Consulate.
Their doctor put the stethoscope on cold
tested me for TB, HIV and syphilis.
Cost, $125 cash.

The final page of the last form asked,
Has your marriage been consummated? Yes or No

Are you planning to overthrow the government
of the United States? Yes or No

I was shaking
when we were called to the window
for our exit interview.
How did you meet?
Who married you?
What's your husband's shoe size?

Outside our Toyota Tercel waited, crammed
with everything we owned.
Mike's new job started in the morning.

On the way out I used the pay phone to call Dad
Good news. You don't have to come get me.

FENCES II

FENCES II

Yesterday two rams broke
through the barbed wire
and wandered the woods
farther and farther.
Forced to trespass for hours, I shook
a bucket of feed, calling *Merlin, Odie.*
Had my old roommate Becca been here
she would have told me when to stop,
knowing they'd come home, come dark.

In Durango she layers colors
on wooden panels,
then sands, scratches, repeats.
Painted fences, corralled sunlight, red climbing hills.

She says when two fences don't meet,
the space between is called no man's land.
No one owns it; anyone can use it.
But I prefer to stay inside my fences,
patch holes, latch gates,
walk narrow, well-worn paths.

Becca's split rail fences
meander like bands of preschoolers
holding hands on a field trip.
They wander into pockets of sky,
become transparent.

She calls her collection *Boundaries*
but her fences keep nothing out
      nothing in.

VOICES

The bearded poet says the voice I need will find me.

When it does I'll take dictation,
write thirty poems before lunch like Gregory Orr.

      But suppose it speaks French or Italian
      or Pennsylvania Dutch?
      What if it has a lisp or st-st-st-utters
      or yells like a border guard
      confiscating moonshine?

What if it develops Alzheimer's
and asks me to take it home again and again and again?

      What if the voice gets a body
      and tries to kiss me?
      You cannot report this stuff.
      Only great authors and saints
      make such confessions.

What if the voice is God?
      What if it isn't?

I do not want to hear the voice
   but I would like to knit thick wooly poems
   that could fix great ills or boredom.

Imagine the voice never comes
and all my poems are just that, the poems

of a middle-aged Mennonite woman
who stayed on the farm.

Perhaps the bearded poet uses the voice as a trick
to make me believe I am not worthy of revelation.

If it comes, I pray it will be like Grandma Martin's
ready with a little joke
and homemade apple fritters
and a thick slice of belief.

POETRY BEFORE BREAKFAST

In that wavery time after waking
before the ordinary day begins,
I write.

My good dog, who smells like the woods,
lies on his yellow-grey back
stretching impossibly long
as I scratch his belly.

For warm up I read Steve Scafidi's
poem "The Egg Suckers," then Jeff Gundy's
"Astonishing Details of the Universe."
While I write Paul Simon sings me to Graceland
and my English Breakfast Tea with cream
steams the morning.

In grade school I chewed my hair
pretending no one could see me.

The damp taste of fear has gone now
and my thoughts don't halt and stutter
but rise sure as the sun.

A voice flows through me:
Will you go further?
This is not an accusation,
not a direction.

Yes, I answer.

BLOWING DANDELION SEEDS

This is how a wish is made.

Wade figurines: green sea turtle, brown beaver—
   now gone—
prizes found in boxes of Red Rose tea.

Three sisters leapt from bed to bed
over a river of beige carpet, full of alligators.

When our mood rings turned violet we told wild stories.

Truth-or-Dare lived under the pine tree tall as knowledge.

After supper, *Hide-and-Seek*,
safety on Mrs. Frey's back stoop.

Now I look everywhere for that little girl.

That wonder can't be lost forever.

Tomorrow white-throated sparrows
will help me find it again.

COME QUIET YOURSELF

You never sit on my bench anymore—
I wait; you pass.

Your husband sawed, drilled, nailed,
propped me with rocks, in front of the pond,

tied a red bow to my seat
and walked you to me in the sun.

You knelt, palms up and
ready, your golden retriever

rippling the water, then shaking off on us.
Now all your Thich Nhat Hanh books lie

shut and lonely, like you.
You think I don't hear your prayers?

Once I stood in the forest,
made and cleaned the air.

If windows face trees, hospital patients heal faster,
feel less pain, go home sooner.

You hide under barn jackets,
high school jeans, as if ready

for muck, the slide of joy,
but you are stingy with your soul.

You want peace without work,
miracles without roots.

I am pine, slow-growing, resistant
to drought, thriving almost anywhere,

as you could.

DOING DISHES

Thich Nhat Hanh teaches
Do dishes as if it's a ceremony,
a rite. Don't hurry,
don't let your thoughts wander,
    and I'm trying,
my sleeves wet and soapy.

But my mind's stuck in yesterday

watching my boss stalk by
to mock his spoiled workers
who want their checks on time.
He huffs down the sidewalk,
bumps the panic button twice
before his doors unlock,
then squeals away
in his red Mustang—.

Your boss is not evil
and does not govern your happiness.
    He is broken.
        Do not cut yourself.

I slide my hands in the slippery water,
watch the dirt dissolve from the hand-blown
glasses that gleam green in the sunlight.

I wring out the dishcloth my mother knit,
remember her saying,

Leave the bullies at the playground.
They hurt because they are hurt.
Go outside, enjoy the day.

Steam rises from the flatware,
the blue plate my husband loves
drips in the drainer
bluer and bluer.

BROTHER LAWRENCE AND THE SHEEP

Eight a.m. I stumble to the barn
in my old high school stoner jacket
with the missing black buttons.
The weeds no one ever seems to pull
or hoe or mind sway in the grass,
wild as my boss in a temper tantrum.

In the warming sunlight, fat borer bees
begin to chew holes in the rafters,
like the board members who took away
Good Friday as a holiday. I swat
them with that tennis racquet
that lies on the hay bale, feel the satisfying thud,
watch the stunned bodies in the dirt winding down.

I sweep manure from mangers,
clatter the feed can and the flock flows into the barn.
They rise, plant their front feet in the troughs,
throw their heads heavenward,
a bleating hungry choir.
I tap my metal scoop, raise it like a baton
and sing my old Sunday School song about patience.
As choir director, I should commit to the words.

It's been years since I sat inside the barn
waiting for a lamb to sniff my legs,
cock his head, one ear drooping with the weight
of a yellow ear tag —
waiting for the ewes to take me in,
to plop down almost near and chew their cuds.

It's just chores now.
I imagine Brother Lawrence hanging his head
as he creaks through the weathered walls,
Practice the presence of God, he chants,
If I could doing dishes, you can tending sheep.

But I'm no monk, I retort.
Unlike you I have a real job, and my boss,
he doesn't give a shit about poetry,
or barns, let alone my soul, and I'm late.
I hurry back to the house, Larry one step
behind, reciting a homily on holy habits.
I plug my ears, change jeans, gulp coffee.

Larry shakes his head as I zoom down the lane,
God is everywhere, he heralds over the fence,
It'd make the day easier if you'd start
by saying hello.

A BLESSING FOR POETS

May a poem find you before breakfast.

May the bees forever make honey for your tea.
    May it stay warm
        while you refine the last line.

May you never fear the quiet,
    the empty page,
    your reader,
    your brother, the editor.
    Rejection will come; don't mope all day.

Write your truth,
lose control,
keep your hand moving.

Invite the muse
    though she's torn
        a thousand invitations.

Kiss your internal censor goodnight
keep him asleep
until the third draft.

Recite your poems to your dog,
your lover, the neighbor,
the purple-haired cashier at the grocery store.

Call your grandma.
If you have none, find one.
There are always old women keeping the fire.

Slip into the sacred ritual
you and the words
as it was in the beginning
when you found yourself lonely
in bed, with a pen and a notebook.

FENCES III

FIXING THINGS

I can't see God calling someone
to be a financial planner
I said in that poem when I was young and broke.
I'd like one now
to plan for our upcoming vacation
which is making me nauseous.
While researching on the computer yesterday
a sudden warning, flashing, freezing.
Then today the bank teller takes over an hour
to send an international bank wire,
she Googles the IBAN and BIC,
Yahoos the conversion rate.
All five tellers know my twenty-fifth anniversary plans,
me cheering my husband skiing the Birkebeiner,
commemorating those Vikings who in birch bark leggings
cross-country skied 54 km
through treacherous mountains and forests
rescuing baby Haakon, heir to the Norwegian throne.

Two windows over, the frosted brunette says all she got
was a weed whacker and dinner at Philippi Inn.

After three phone calls to her supervisor,
the teller says she can't guarantee the amount
the bank in Norway will receive.
And since it's Friday afternoon
it won't go through today.
She'll be told if there's a problem, probably,
but there's no way to check.

She hopes she filled out the paperwork okay,
tells me to cross my fingers and pray.

I was going to go to the mall tonight.
Generally, I hate trying things on,
but I psyched myself up to buy something
that fits and is in style, to make my husband happy.
He is gone this weekend,
unable to check me into reality.

Saturday, hiking in the woods with my dog,
I stop to pray like the teller ordered.
Cross-legged on the ground I begin, but then the crying.
All I can think of is how my husband will kill me
after we lose thousands of dollars. I am ridiculous.
He is a pacifist, would tell me to stop, but I won't.
I am in detention, writing 100 times on the blackboard,
Cheryl is an idiot.
The rest of the world banks with ease,
plans vacations without ulcers.
The good doctor who died of a brain tumor
said I should pray in tree stands, up in the air,
above things. There are no tree stands here.
Sunday, I do the laundry, bathe the dog,
clean the neighbor's gutters.
But Monday is Labor Day, big, expansive,
and the teller keeps yacking.
I can't write poetry when I can't think
and the chores are all done
so I stay in bed until 4 p.m.
I am supposed to call someone I love

when I am like this. I call my sister,
act casual, complain about rural West Virginia,
mourn the metropolis I left.
Minutes after saying good-bye
her husband calls from his office
overtime prepping for a meeting.
Everything is fixable he tells me,
there's a bigger bank that handles international currency.
He doesn't hang up until I'm calm.
I believe him. He fixed that small broken piece
in my sister, cleans my dog's teeth when he visits,
doesn't yell in a canoe,
and everyone is at ease when he sits at the table.

I was afraid to meet him
after he started dating my sister,
after I wrote that bad thing about his profession
in that poem I was pretty sure my sister
would make him read.
But everything is fixable.

Because in 1206 the King's infant son Haakon was abducted
and two Birkebeiners, named for their birch leggings,
skied through a civil war to save the baby.

Because those two warriors skied through a blizzard,
over mountains, from Lillehammer to Trondheim,
to the throne, cradling little Haakon.

Because it's our twenty-fifth anniversary
and we want to go somewhere.

Because I made it through the winter of 2014.

Because I like to think I could be someone else
in a faraway place.

Because Trump doesn't care if I leave the country
and I don't care if I can't come back.

Because seven thousand skiers will iron-in wax,
cool and scrape, brush and polish,
don eight-pound packs, as if carrying Haakon,
and ski 54 km, the distance to safety.

Because the crowds will dig out snow forts,
carve out couches, cover them in deer skins,
ring cowbells and cheer, "heia, heia, heia."

Because my husband will ski all three Birkies,
the Norwegian, the American, the Canadian,
and receive the Haakon Haakonsson award.

Because peace was restored when Haakon reigned.

Because we share history,
a reason to go forward,
uphill, downhill, to rise after falling.

Because in Norway everyone skis
and they are the happiest people in the world.

OUR CANADIAN BIRKIE

It starts at Carl Dettwiler's farm in 1978
I'm thirteen
our church cross-country skis
through sugar bush and stubbled corn fields.
Next Saturday Dad buys skis
for the whole family.

In 2008 we hear the story of Haakon
and the race to save the prince.
The last week of training Dad gets winded
before learning of his leukemia
but extreme cold preempts my worry
and the Birkie.

In 2020, at 77, Dad wants to try again
so I fly from West Virginia and he from Toronto
to Alberta's aspen forests, lakes and beaver dams,
to winter's clean white fleece.

Race morning the track set glistens,
the air is still, the snow perfect,
the temperature a lovely -11°C.
A moose stands by the side of the road.

People gliding by call,
Good job! Beautiful Day! Keep it Up!

Don, the volunteer rover with a first aid kit
and an extra ski pole strapped to his pack,
checks Dad's bindings and relays updates
if one of us drifts behind the other.

At the rest stop 18 kilometers in,
a woman plays the harmonica
beside a tray of warm Gatorade.

I herringbone up a hill
—pull over to pant.
I drink water from my pack.
When Don comes, I stand straight
steady the swaying horizon
so I don't get pulled from the race.

Dad sings Mendelssohn's Elijah
He that shall endure to the end shall be saved,
and I mumble, *I think I can, I think I can*
like the little engine that could.

With one kilometer left
Don tells Dad
You look fresh as a daisy.

Volunteers dressed as Vikings cheer us
as we push through the finish line
exhausted and triumphant.

WHAT LIES BENEATH

My husband talks bees all morning.

After 9/11 we changed the way we make love.

During the QA meeting my boss nods off four times.
    Later he emails, *Are you mad at me?*

No one comes when I scream in the barn.

A friend tells me two women at the gym envy my figure.

A patient yells, *Write in my chart MS sucks.*

Our rooster crows all day.

Gone three nights, my husband calls
    ten minutes before *Jeopardy* starts.

At church Mrs. Swick baby-talks to men, wants me to wax
    my brows, explain why I miss so much.

There's a humming sound the others don't hear,
    an industrial sound deep in the woods.

I'm waiting.

PANIC ATTACK

My husband leans toward me,
eyes soft as summer,
waiting for me to speak—
wanting to fix me—
as if I am an engine
or leaky faucet,
as if he can wrench the words out
rearrange my thoughts
and piece me back together.

Like someone scratching inside my skull, I cry,
a sharp wind scraping my skin,
a slow-motion funnel cloud, a lightning strike.
My hands, my mind, my stomach
singed pieces flying everywhere
     in the kitchen,
          the living room,
               outside the picture window
wavering above the grass.

Someone tosses me away, piece by piece,
as if it's a game, as if they're in charge,
ordering me to sit down, be quiet.

I like to do as I'm told.
I want to pass.

But I failed grade two and liked it.
Easier the second time, with the new kids

who didn't know about that afternoon I wet my pants
during math. The second year I knew
some answers and waved my arm.

My husband keeps looking at me, keeps probing.
I want him to stop. I don't tell him
how I pulled over on my trip to Elora last fall,
wrote him a letter, instructions, permission
on how and when to leave me.
How I kept it three months in the glove compartment
then tore it up, buried it in gas station trash.

What I do say is all the colors turn off
and my insides jabber and tell lies
and my dark red meat twitches
like I am full of candy bars and coffee,
like I need to sprint around my old high school track
until I collapse.

Meanwhile all the pieces
fly farther and farther
dispersing in the hayfield
slow and impossible as that puzzle
in the back of my second-grade class
my teacher wanted me to finish.

The pieces must fit together.
I gather as many as I can.
I don't know where I begin
        where I end.

My husband and my teacher settle together,
again, at the big desk in the back,
    waiting.

MOSTLY I HATE MY HEAD

with all its dull noise,
        and my stomach
the sputtering, the backing up.

Ginger tea is good for nausea
but I can't stand the smell, the sharp
yellow taste.

I dislike my fast-talking doctor with his sterile
scents and shiny shoes
telling me I don't look depressed,
then six months later correcting me with pills.

I hate not fully disbelieving
        in reincarnation
that I might have to come back
        and do this again.

I hate the wobble of my bicycle tire
going downhill. Riding horses—
that one at Lake Louise who turned
part way up the mountain to chomp
grass over the side of the cliff.

I loathe confident women who look like Christmas
but never unwrap, never crinkle.

It scares me to think my husband would never
leave me even if I turned into someone terrible.

I hate my dad's leukemia,
my aunt's uncertainties, my cousin's crying,
Grandpa Bauman's breakdown
back in 1952.

I hate my throat, the long distance
from thought to voice,
the lost words.

I hate the virgin births of Greek gods,
the extinction of passenger pigeons,
the slow growth of blueberry bushes

empty Saturdays when I should write
but don't,

that dream, that watery house, my hand
turning the doorknob without invitation,
inside all my peers
lounging with coffee and cushions,
discussing things of great consequence.

I hate the throbbing
from that small dark spot on my neck
and no one coming
        to suck out the poison
            and spit.

RATTLED

The universe recites the same truths
    over and over
a soft, sweet refrain
but I make such a *racket* I can't hear.
Even when I quiet, voices from the TV and radio
    wander through my thoughts.

I obsess over retirement, security.
The money I think I need would make a thousand
people happy in another country.

A man in Kenya, when asked
what would give him joy for life
replied, *My own mango tree, a bit of land,*
a mud hut with a thatch roof.

I once asked my sister,
    if I can't make it....

And she said yes, she'd take me in.
I've always wanted an escape route
ever since the neighbor boy didn't marry me,
ever since that prof told me the school
almost didn't accept me.

I didn't think I'd last this long,
but I have traces of stars in my cells,
stars that when I was a girl
whispered to me a secret

that sifted through the noise of the playground
whose echo, faint, persistent,
I still can't decipher—or forget.

NIGHT IS EASY

Often during the day I think
this too will end in bed.
Almost all my days have ended in bed.
I love bed—
no doctors, no patients, no instructions,
no small talk, no audits.
Just the snores of my husband or the call
of our confused Polish rooster.

Wearing only my mother's wool socks
I flop, stretch, tuck,
pull my patchwork tighter
around my thought-congested chest.
I soften under my turquoise quilt,
under black embroidered names:
all those women from church who cried
when God sent Grandma to The States.

Scattered across the floor,
books of poems with a wood-paneled
station wagon heading west,
and a boy playing his violin on the hillside,
and a brown bear in a top hat.
The moon hums a lullaby
from window to window
as I take the bear's hand and wander the woods.

RECALCULATING

After reading *Born to Run*
I jog down the slope of my drive
gravel and dirt under my feet
remembering the sound of my old cross-country coach
cheering me on.

When I reach the pond with two mallards
I imagine myself twenty years older
and by the time I pant past the Holsteins
I can picture myself in the nursing home
as a resident, not that innocent fourteen-year-old
in white stockings, working the dumb waiter.

Running past Skunk Hollow I wonder
what if I had married that forest ranger in Colorado,
quit nursing school, got my M.F.A.?

My husband doesn't like my new puzzle wedding ring,
three copper pieces you can weave and unweave.
He called it ornate.
I called the plain silver band utilitarian.
He lost his while running,
waited two months to replace it.
Maybe he wants to love someone else.

Just before the slouched, yellow trailer
with a choir of baritone hounds in the yard, I turn around.

Forty-five

I should have written something magnificent by now,
been in library newspapers, had critiques, Oprah calling.
I should have gone wild like my brother-in-law,
tattoos and go-cart racing.

Mortality nips at my heels
as I cut through the woods
the path full of sunken cow prints
downed barbed wire in the grass.

Most of my friends are reinventing themselves,
climbing rock faces, running marathons,
and my old roommate is learning to drive a Harley
in her forties.

Even my father is sloughing off singed skin
from hell-fire sermons, sickness and accidents.
He is lying on a beach in Cuba, wearing Elvis sunglasses,
reading *The Kite Runner*, watching girls.
Watching girls!

I know I never should have stopped
running after high school.
Once home I stretch my legs, my sides, my thoughts
of tomorrow.

Overnight three new age spots blossom
under my right eye, like tears.

THE TROUBLE WITH STYLISTS

They talk—
daughters running for Fair Queen,
strapless gowns and stilettos,
what teacher did what for no good reason,
whose husbands cheat and why.
I don't know how to enter this talk, how to stop it.

Years ago, when smoking was still in vogue
a stylist lit a cigarette
curled the white smoke above my head.
She had scissors.
I said nothing
    Nothing
while she, tethered to a coiled phone cord,
orchestrated rides, childcare, dinner duties.

Why can't beauty be quiet,
like meditation or prayer,
    incense burning for us, the divine
        in our grey plastic capes.

I want a poet to color my hair,
to be her only friend for this hour.
She could talk Bible stories, folktales, myths,
the old knowing, women intuitive and brave,
as her hands scrub my scalp.

I don't like to think myself vain.
I asked my sister and she said

I can dye my hair another eight years.
It took almost two to find medium ash blonde.
I've dreamt of going platinum,
eyebrow wax and manicures.

My stylist asks if I need a little glitter in the hair gel

as if this is ordinary

me fifty and dreaming of being a Breck Girl
on the back cover of *Seventeen*.

FENCES *III*

When the ground is yielding but not muddy
we gather locust posts,
a giant spool of barbed wire,
a pail of silver staples,
and that tool that twists or pulls out mistakes.
My head unravels last night's dream:
a strange man, a river, a city I never lived in.

Newly married
I'd pack a thermos of coffee
and homemade sour cream cookies,
as if it were a holiday to work with you.
Now I bring water, some pretzels.

The Massey Ferguson mutters
and black clots belch from the tailpipe.
Our good dog runs ahead,
ears and tongue flapping like laundry.
You gave him to me when I was sad
and couldn't say why.

You stand in the bucket and instruct.
I sit in the driver's seat, try to listen
without shaking, my hand on the lever where
up is down, down is up
left and right level and spill.
At your ideal spot, I hop out,
hold the post steady while you drive it down
with a black iron maul

big enough to crush my skull if you miss.
    This is trust,
            and I do,
despite those teenage girls you jog with at six a.m.

I don't run anymore
and I lust for things I never used to,
hammered silver and green turquoise rings.
You say I don't need them; I should let my hair go grey,
be natural, how I used to be. I don't say,
there are scars across my belly
and my skin is loosening.
    I need something shiny.

You come to all my readings,
ask for a poem as prayer before meals, before company.

But there's no money in poetry.

You want me with a real job
so I won't get bored or become a hermit.

I want you with a real job, too,
one not related to the church or the poor,
one that would give us health insurance,
let me stay home to write similes and metaphors,
but you won't work for *the evil empire*.

After each post is planted, I squint one eye,
look down the line.

This fence work never gets done—
storms will loosen and crack it,
tree limbs will fall,
a ram will reach his neck through the wires
to nibble a briar leaf,
a ewe will leap over—

still we stretch the barbed wire
as if we can keep anything from wandering,
the coyotes from slipping in.

It's like the moment before you faint.
Before the cut starts to bleed.

Like the screeching of the kettle and the stove
    inching away from your hand.

It's like diving under water and forgetting
    how to surface.

Like tripping over a rock,
    the hillside lengthening.

Like counting three lambs when there should be four.

It's like someone yelling in the grocery store
Stay away from me
and you realize it's you.

It's like risking your life for a Frosty,
the teenage cashier in the drive-thru,
glove-less, bare-faced.

It's like that.
Except it never happens.

And then it does.

COVID-19 REWINDS

I wish I had written an online review
for the young girl at Subway,
with red hair like my sister's.
I should have praised how quickly
and competently she made my roast beef,
cut the bread in the center,
and zigzagged the dressing.
She understood half hour lunches,
unlike her coworkers.

Often she worked ten days in a row,
as others quit or called off or got fired.

After filling my sandwich orders for a week,
she suggested I shampoo with cold water
to keep my curls from frizzing.
She asked what I did for fun,
how my writing was going.

At 3:20 she'd duck out smiling
to the bus stop, pick up her two kids,
and race them back to the restaurant laughing.
She bought them juice, helped start their homework.

Now the streets are empty,
Chairs hang upside down from tabletops
as I walk by the window,
hungry, missing her voice.

COVID-19 BEAUTY LESSONS

My stylist smiles warm as the sun
and smells of lavender after the rain.

When I first moved here
she gave me advice on cooking venison
and getting to know my neighbors.
I trust her with more than my hair.

She's the only person in town
I told about my brother-in-law,
how he chose to live on the street
those last few months,
how he died on Mount Mackenzie
in winter, a Bible in his hand.

She streaked my hair young
for that photo on my last book.

Sometimes while straightening my hair
she'd laugh and swap stories
with other customers, longtime friends
talking high school.

Once I wrote a mean poem about her.
Now I realize I just felt left out and awkward,
jealous of her easy banter.
I wish I'd tipped better
at my last appointment.

Today her shop's empty.
In the window a tuxedoed teddy bear
a homemade mask over his mouth and nose
a giant paw raised in hello.

COVID-19 REGRETS

I

I never thanked Beatrice
my babysitter for writing letters
to Mom in the hospital as if from me
telling how I baked a chocolate cake
in the Easy-Bake Oven and learned
to play Checkers.

II

I didn't buy flowers for Uncle Mark
and Aunt Edith although they renovated
the front room so I could stay for nursing school.
He had their boys walk me to campus the first day
and she made dozens of butterscotch squares.

III

Instead of happy anticipation
for my cousins' visit to the farm,
I worried what they'd think
of our steep driveway
the ladybugs on the living room window,
the mouse trap in the cupboard.

IV

When I was in VS* in Colorado
the boy who planned to marry me
flew with my parents for a weeklong visit
and I dumped him the first night.
Even though three months earlier we'd registered

our favorite china pattern and talked about kids.
Mom wrote him a letter saying she was sorry.
I never did.

VS—Mennonite Voluntary Service

WEDDING CHINA

For twenty years my husband
had been eating off my old boyfriend's plates,
Daybreak by Denby, sturdy white daises,
Tim and I picked before I left for VS.
Mom sent us to the House of China
expecting an engagement
as soon as my term in Colorado ended.

In twenty years Mike had broken only one bowl.
Our brother-in-law, at dinner, learning the history,
hooted and hollered, wondered how long
Mike had to dine with Tim's plates. Mom's guilt sprouted.
For our next anniversary she laughed, handed us a card
blossoming with bills, *for Mike to find a new pattern.*
He chose Fiesta's deep blue.
But we kept the old meat platter,
the casserole dish,
the saltshaker,
being practical,
used to such things.

SWALLOWING

In Mrs. Ellis' class when it was time for our test
with that giant clown poster with all the colors
we were supposed to know
I got stomach sick
 that easy-to-slip-into sick
 that struck again in Nursing school,
 the 6 a.m. vomiting
 then walking erect,
blue pinstripes, that white starched cap.
During med pass my hands shook, breaking
the glass vial of dilaudid,
cutting my palm.
In Peds all those tiny calculations
and that boy with his gangrenous foot,
me mixing powders and solutions,
hanging little IV bags, counting drops,
questioning my math, interrupting my sleep.

When I was twenty-five and freshly engaged
my future aunt asked *lemonade or iced tea?*
and I turned to my fiancé for the answer.
Drank the tea I did not like.

After the open mic reading
the poet I love danced
right in front of the guitar man.
My legs ached to join her but stood
like pillars immobile before the whiskey
breath prof criticizing my poems, standing so close

like he might kiss me while I swallowed
the words I wanted to scream.

At forty-five, I was going to be the only
nurse in the county making home visits by motorcycle.
On a tiny toy Honda I drew
giant figure eights in the field, then graduated to dirt
roads. But I imagined men in pick-up trucks laughing
at my efforts. And then that slight incline, that rose
like Everest, while I whispered *fuck, fuck,*
fuck, under my helmet
before placing an ad in *The Trader:*
One slightly used Honda 200.

Someday I'll be ninety-five, and a porcelain-
skinned nurse will enter my room without knocking,
hand me a small paper cup with two oval pink pills and one
    blue.
    I will think
    these are not
    mine.
She will hand me a glass of water, confident
in her white uniform, shiny nametag,
shimmery smile. I will hesitate.
    She'll nod.
    I'll shake
the pills onto my tongue,
        swallow.

WHAT SUSTAINS ME

The long line of horse-and-buggies
that clip-clop to church Sunday mornings
sound like tree frogs on the hillside.

Red-tails riding thermals while four poets
on the porch prune their metaphors.

Mom's bearhug and laughter when I was a girl,
when I asked why Grandpa, who was normally happy,
yelled when he preached, madly shaking his fist.

The bright pompoms tying the black shawls
of Old Order women, that one autumn
when they were allowed a dollop of color:
lime green, McIntosh red,
orange, fuchsia and turquoise.

An old dog asleep in a sunbeam.

The Indian tribe that says all creation stories are true.

The bearded man who says many creation stories
start with revenge, battles and poison,
but ours starts with a word, a breath.

The Egyptian prof who buys a lamb to remember
Abraham's willingness to sacrifice his son.
He chooses our best,
binds the lamb's legs with electrical tape,
gently heaves him into the trunk of his BMW.

Early morning fog rolling off the pond.

My husband who turns the sanctuary into a woodshop.
For Sunday worship we build houses for barred owls.

My 105-year-old Grandma
in her apartment
singing hymns.

WHAT I'VE LEARNED FROM MY PARENTS

to be content collecting a dish pattern from Texaco,
to turn a chicken coop into Bauman Printing,
to refashion a wedding gown into a skirt for a bassinet,

to know the call of a cardinal,

that a home needs classical music, 96.3,
whether anyone is listening or not,

that cross-country skiing
trumps work, trumps almost anything,

that it's important to listen,
listen, if someone is eroding
let him sleep in the basement,
invite him to choir practice,

to always carry hard candy in my pockets,

to soften a daughter's failure
with French fries and gravy,

to shingle the roof side by side
with the guy who tried to rob your shop,

to say *God is Great and God is Good*, to lie on the floor ready
to give plane rides, to tuck three girls into bed,
then go quietly
    back to work.

I learned to baste a turkey with ginger ale and not cry
if the green beans fall on the floor,

to sing Elvis Presley and shake my hips
at Christmas, without wine or spiked eggnog,

to find homes for boat people from Laos,

that beginnings can flare wearing horsehair
crinoline, saddle shoes and Brylcreem,
that love can fill fifty years and more.

AGAIN WITH THE SHEEP

Today the calendar says, *Write Poetry,*
before getting up, before
leaving that watery time.
But outside my bedroom window
two sheep are on the wrong side of the fence
as if the fence were just a suggestion.
This is a community farm
but the men are gone.
The men are always gone when the sheep get out.
Shutting my notebook
I plunge my feet in black boots
and trudge to the barn,
find the feed can empty.
Buddha says breathe deep, even, gentle.
I try.   *Damn men.*

I shake a small bribe in a yellow bucket,
yell, *Sarah, Sarah.* I call every ewe Sarah
after the good one, that Suffolk
who went to market years ago.
She ate from our hands,
led the flock wherever we said.

Again I jostle the feed
and the two impudent ewes fling up their faces
and take off bleating, chasing me to the barn
but at the open door they stop. Understanding
the trick,   they stomp,   turn,
dirty wool-balls bound down the field.

Panting, I phone Minnette: *Sheep, out, tried, can't.*
She comes in her magical calm
and the ewes, as if deciding she is the Good Shepherd,
trot into the barn behind her.
With that done we walk the fence line
search for holes, tufts of pulled wool on barbed wire.
I apologize for interrupting her morning.
She laughs, *It is what it is,* her mantra
for anything that goes awry.

Unable to leave, I sit watching the flock
and they watch me.
    I am dissolving
into the wide black slots of their pupils.
With hard yellow teeth they yank clumps of grass.
Jaws jut side to side. They baaa
as if their mouths are full of marbles,
as if to say we are content and intend to stay.
With that they send me home.

ACKNOWLEDGMENTS

Thank you to the magazines, books, and projects where some of these poems first appeared or were recorded, sometimes in slightly different versions:

In *Fluent* online magazine ed. Nancy McKeithen
"Where I'm From," Oct.-Nov. 2013
"Recalculating," Aug.-Sept. 2013
"Inheritance," Winter 2015
"Come Quiet Yourself," Winter 2015

In *Sheila-Na-Gig* online magazine ed. Hayley Mitchell Haugen
"Fences," "Again with the Sheep," volume 1, Fall 2016
"Fixing Things," and "Panic Attack," volume 1.4, Summer 2017
"Recurring Dream," volume 3.4, Summer 2019
"What Sustains Me," volume 5.1, Fall 2020

In *Hamilton Stone Review* online magazine, ed. Lynda Schor and Kevin Stein
"Fences III," issue 45, Fall 2021

In the *Anthology of Appalachian Writers*, with Nikki Giovanni, vol. VIII, 2016
"Recurring Dream"
"Again with the Sheep"
An earlier version of "Not a Bedtime Story"

In *Backbone Mountain Review, Literary Review,2016*, ed. Jennifer Merrifield, published by the Allegheny Arts Council, the Allegany County Library System, and the Frostburg Center for Literary Arts, with assistance of Frostburg State University, the

Community Trust Foundation, and NewPage Corporation.
"A Script of Seven Days," 40.

In *The Raconteur Review* online magazine, volume 1, issue 1
"April 2020"
"COVID-19 Beauty Lessons"
"COVID-19 Regrets"

In *Eyes Glowing at the Edge of the Woods, fiction and poetry from West Virginia*, eds. Laura Long and Doug Van Gundy, Vandalia Press, Morgantown, 2017.
"Waking to Spring," 64-65.

In *Feminine Rising, Voices of Power and Invisibility* eds. Andrea Fekete and Lara Lillibridge, Cynren Press, Malvern, PA, 2019.
"Swallowing," 198-199.

In *Pathways, Poetry and Prose by the Barbour County Writers' Workshop*. eds., Cheryl Denise and Anni L. Corley, Philippi, WV 2015.
"Waking to Spring," 1
"Inheritance," 16-17
"Recalculating," 34-35
"Come Quiet Yourself,"48-49
"What I've Learned from My Parents," 63-64.

In *Pine Mountain Sand & Gravel, Appalachia Acting Up*, eds. Paulette Hansel, Michael Henson and Sherry Cook Stanforth, vol. 21, 2018.
"The Boy from Down the Hill," 110-112.

In *Voices from the Attic,* ed. Jan Beatty, Carlow University Press, Pittsburgh, PA, 2015.
"Mostly I Hate My Head," 83-84, an earlier version of "The Girl Inside the Woman," 85-86.

In *Women on the Line* A Collection of poems, Athens, Ohio, 2015.
"Blowing Dandelion Seeds," 10.

In *Women Speak*, eds., Kari Gunter-Seymour and Kristine Williams, Women of Appalachia Project, 2017.
"Fences II," 6.

In *Women Speak*, eds., Kari Gunter-Seymour and Kristine Williams, vol. 3, Women of Appalachia Project, 2018.
"The Boy from Down the Hill," 14-15.

In *Women Speak, 10th Anniversary Collection*, ed. Kristine Williams, vol. 4, Women of Appalachia Project, 2019.
An earlier version of "The Trouble with Stylists," 117-118.

In the digital exhibit of *West Virginias' Creative Response to COVID-19 Folklife Program Blog*, wvfolklife.org/2021/06/09
"COVID-19 Beauty Lessons"

Recorded for *Poetry Spoken Here* podcast with host Charlie Rossiter and producer/technical director Jack Rossiter-Munley, episode #80, Nov. 2018
"Panic Attack"
"Brother Lawrence and the Sheep"
"Again with the Sheep"
"Fences II"

Recorded for *Poetry During A Time of Crisis,* an online project
of the WV Humanities Council 2020.
"Where I'm From"

Cheryl Denise grew up in Elmira, Ontario. She went to the red brick Mennonite church next to the white clapboard Old Order Meetinghouse. In winter she along with neighbor kids skated on the ice of flooded backyards and made snow forts, and the rest of the year she played hide-and-seek for hours. At fourteen she started working after school at the Elmira Nursing Home.

After graduating from nursing school, she worked three years as a volunteer public health nurse in La Jara, Colorado. She fell for her future husband while helping to make suppers at the Homeless Shelter where he was volunteering. They moved to Philippi, West Virginia, and became leaders for the Mennonite Service Adventure program for three years, living with teens and instilling values of community service.

Now they live in the intentional community of Shepherds Field in a timber framed home they built themselves. Cheryl works as a nurse with seniors and disabled persons. She enjoys biking, hiking and cross-country skiing with Mike and their good dog, Birkie.